J

ALL AROUND THE WORLD
IRELAND

by Jessica Dean

pogo

Ideas for Parents and Teachers

Pogo Books let children practice reading informational text while introducing them to nonfiction features such as headings, labels, sidebars, maps, and diagrams, as well as a table of contents, glossary, and index.

Carefully leveled text with a strong photo match offers early fluent readers the support they need to succeed.

Before Reading

- "Walk" through the book and point out the various nonfiction features. Ask the student what purpose each feature serves.
- Look at the glossary together. Read and discuss the words.

Read the Book

- Have the child read the book independently.
- Invite him or her to list questions that arise from reading.

After Reading

- Discuss the child's questions. Talk about how he or she might find answers to those questions.
- Prompt the child to think more. Ask: Ireland is known as the Emerald Isle. Is there a nickname for the area where you live?

Pogo Books are published by Jump!
5357 Penn Avenue South
Minneapolis, MN 55419
www.jumplibrary.com

Copyright © 2019 Jump!
International copyright reserved in all countries. No part of this book may be reproduced in any form without written permission from the publisher.

Library of Congress Cataloging-in-Publication Data

Names: Dean, Jessica, 1963- author.
Title: Ireland / by Jessica Dean.
Description: Pogo books.
Minneapolis, MN : Jump!, Inc., [2019]
Series: All around the world | Includes index.
Audience: Ages 7-10.
Identifiers: LCCN 2018018935 (print)
LCCN 2018020424 (ebook)
ISBN 9781641281669 (ebook)
ISBN 9781641281645 (hardcover : alk. paper)
ISBN 9781641281652 (pbk.)
Subjects: LCSH: Ireland—Juvenile literature.
Classification: LCC DA906 (ebook)
LCC DA906 .D46 2019 (print) | DDC 941.7—dc23
LC record available at https://lccn.loc.gov/2018018935

Editor: Kristine Spanier
Designer: Molly Ballanger

Photo Credits: Patryk Kosmider/Shutterstock, cover; Maria Burmistrova/Shutterstock, 1; Pixfiction/Shutterstock, 3; Krzysztof Nahlik/iStock, 4; shutterupeire/Shutterstock, 5 (landscape); AndreAnita/Shutterstock, 5 (puffin); Shay Culligan/SuperStock, 6-7; J Orr/Alamy, 8-9; Mustang_79/iStock, 10; Dougall_Photography/iStock, 11; SteveAllenPhoto/iStock, 12-13; Hemis/SuperStock, 14-15; Food and Drink/SuperStock, 16; vm2002/Shutterstock, 17; konstantinks/Shutterstock, 18-19; Ramsey Cardy/Getty, 20-21; RomanR/Shutterstock, 23.

Printed in the United States of America at Corporate Graphics in North Mankato, Minnesota.

TABLE OF CONTENTS

CHAPTER 1

WELCOME TO IRELAND!

Visit old castles. Snack on soda bread and tea. Kiss the Blarney Stone. Welcome to Ireland!

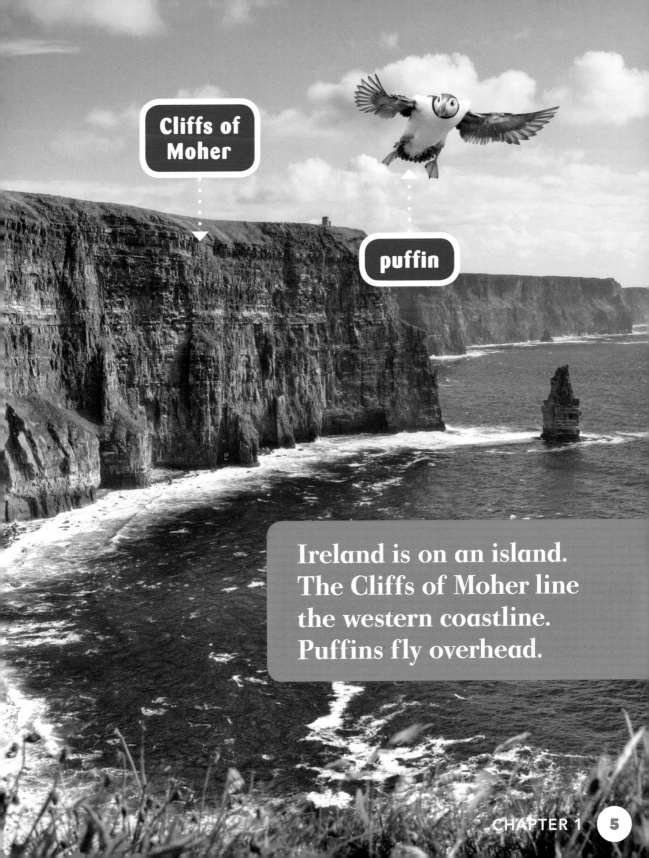

Cliffs of Moher

puffin

Ireland is on an island.
The Cliffs of Moher line
the western coastline.
Puffins fly overhead.

The **Celts** lived in Ireland more than 2,000 years ago. The Vikings **invaded** the island. When? In 795. Armies from other lands followed. England took over in 1171.

Ireland became fully **independent** in 1949. Dublin is the **capital**. Lawmakers meet in the Leinster House.

WHAT DO YOU THINK?

Ireland used to be ruled by the United Kingdom. Northern Ireland is still part of the United Kingdom. Some people want Northern Ireland to rejoin Ireland. How do you think Northern Ireland should decide which country to be part of?

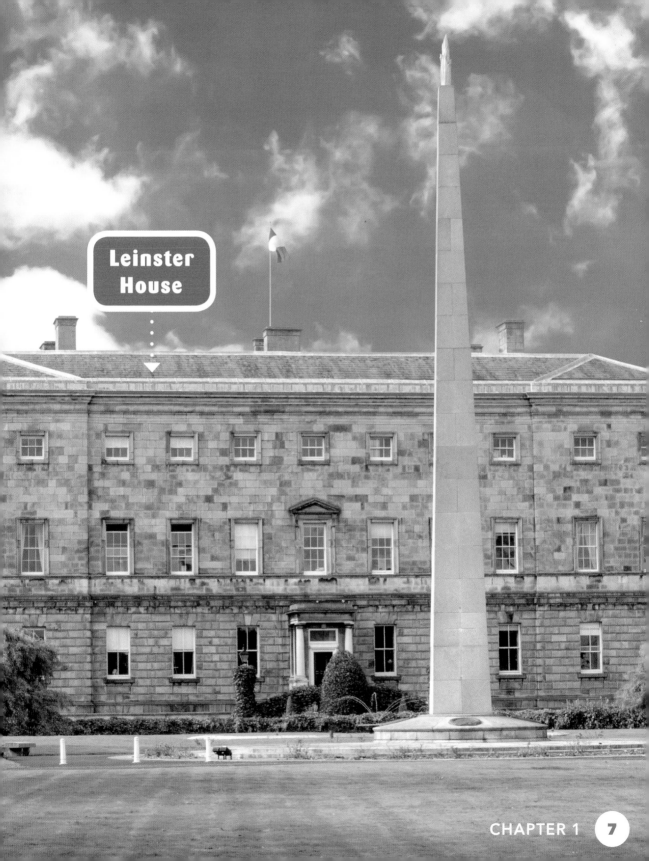

Leinster House

cabbage

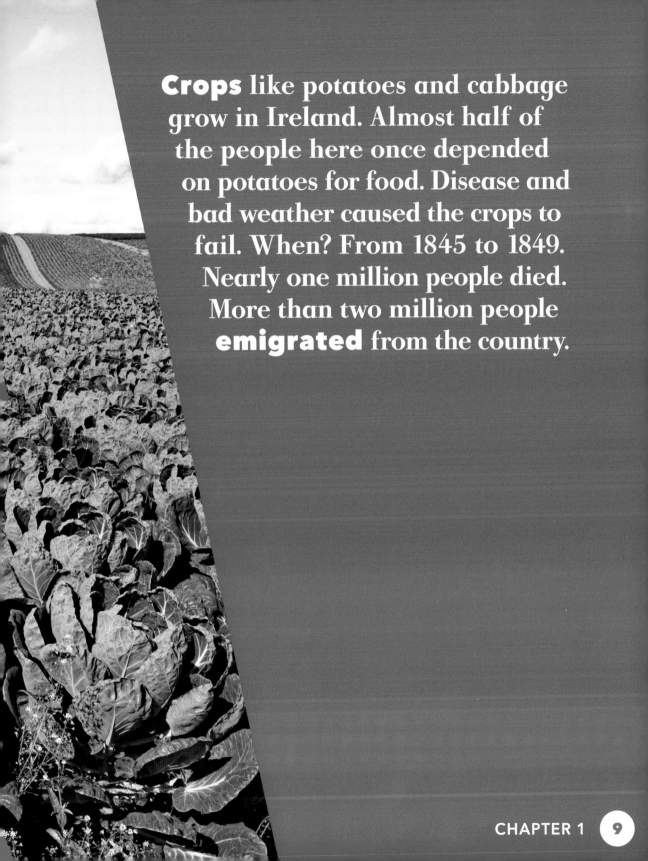

Crops like potatoes and cabbage grow in Ireland. Almost half of the people here once depended on potatoes for food. Disease and bad weather caused the crops to fail. When? From 1845 to 1849. Nearly one million people died. More than two million people **emigrated** from the country.

CHAPTER 2

LIFE IN IRELAND

The country is called the Emerald Isle. Why? It is so green! It is perfect for raising **livestock**. In fact, there are more sheep than people here.

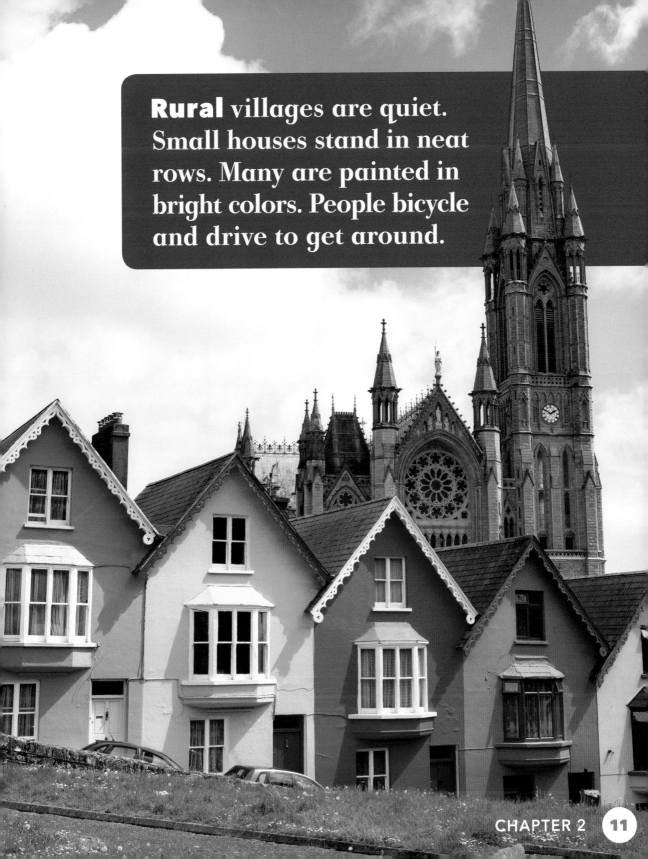

Rural villages are quiet. Small houses stand in neat rows. Many are painted in bright colors. People bicycle and drive to get around.

Cork is a city in Ireland. Blarney Castle is here. This **fortress** was built in 1446. The Blarney Stone is wedged up high. Visitors kiss it. Why? **Folklore** says the stone has magical powers. People believe they will get the "gift of **gab**" from kissing it.

DID YOU KNOW?

The Blarney Stone may be half of the original Stone of Scone. The first king of Scots sat upon it when he became king. When? In the 800s!

Blarney Castle

Children here must go to school from the age of six to 15 years old. Do they want to go to college? They stay in school three more years to prepare if they do. Students learn the Irish language at school.

WHAT DO YOU THINK?

One third of the schools here are for only boys or only girls. Do you go to a school like that? What do you think it would it be like if you did? Would you like it? Why or why not?

CHAPTER 3

FOOD AND FUN

Start the day with a soft egg on toast. Lunch is a hearty stew. For dinner, meat is served with carrots and potatoes. A favorite dish is called colcannon. It is mashed potatoes and cabbage.

colcannon ····▶

tea

Irish soda bread is served with many meals. A favorite beverage is tea. Even children drink it!

soda bread

Singing folk songs. Dancing. Telling stories of the past. These are all important here. Irish dancers twirl and kick. Their heels clack out a strong rhythm. Arms are straight by their sides. It is harder than it looks!

TAKE A LOOK!

The arrival of the Celts marked the beginning of Irish music. What traditional instruments do musicians still play here?

accordion

bodhrán

bouzouki

Celtic harp

fiddle

flute

harmonica

tin whistle

Hurling is popular. It is a high-speed sport like field hockey. Gaelic football is a cross between soccer and rugby. Many play handball. People also hike, fish, and swim.

There is so much to do on the Emerald Isle. What would you like to do here?

hurling

QUICK FACTS & TOOLS

IRELAND

Location: Island off northwestern Europe

Size: 27,133 square miles (70,273 square kilometers)

Population: 5,011,102 (July 2017 estimate)

Capital: Dublin

Type of Government: parliamentary republic

Languages: English and Irish

Exports: machinery, computers, chemicals, food, animal products

Currency: euro

capital: A city where government leaders meet.

Celts: People who were living in Ireland during the Iron Age.

crops: Plants grown for food.

emigrated: To have left one's home country to live in another country.

folklore: The stories, customs, and beliefs of the common people that are handed down from one generation to the next.

fortress: A place that is fortified against attack.

gab: To chat.

independent: Free from a controlling authority.

invaded: Entered a place in order to occupy or control it.

livestock: Animals that are kept or raised on a farm or ranch.

rural: Related to the country and country life.

Ireland's currency

INDEX

TO LEARN MORE

Learning more is as easy as 1, 2, 3.

1) Go to www.factsurfer.com

2) Enter "Ireland" into the search box.

3) Click the "Surf" button to see a list of websites.

With factsurfer, finding more information is just a click away.